Maine

in Four Seasons

Maine
in Four Seasons

20
Poets
Celebrate
the
Turning
Year

Edited by Wesley McNair
Illustrated by Jan Owen

Down East

Copyright © 2010 by Wesley McNair
Illustrations © 2010 by Jan Owen
Individual poems copyright by poet
Used with permission
All rights reserved

ISBN: 978-0-89272-815-2

BOOKS·MAGAZINE·ONLINE
www.downeast.com

Design by Lynda Chilton

Printed in China

5   4   3   2   1

Distributed to the trade by National Book Network

Library of Congress Cataloging-in-Publication Data

Maine in four seasons : 20 poets celebrate the turning year / edited by
Wesley McNair ; illustrated by Jan Owen.
    p. cm.
  ISBN 978-0-89272-815-2 (alk. paper)
  1. Maine--Poetry. 2. Seasons--Maine--Poetry. 3. American poetry--
Maine. I. McNair, Wesley.
  PS595.M25M35 2010
  811.008'09741--dc22
                        2009043760

Acknowledgments

Kate Barnes: "Sometimes," from *Kneeling Orion* by Kate Barnes. Copyright © 2004 by Kate Barnes. Reprinted by permission of David R. Godine, Publisher, Inc.

Louise Bogan: "The Dragonfly," from *The Blue Estuaries* by Louise Bogan. Copyright © 1968 by Louise Bogan. Copyright renewed 1996 by Ruth Limmer. Reprinted by permission of Farrar, Straus and Giroux, LLC.

Philip Booth: "Civilities," from *Lifelines* by Philip Booth. Copyright © 1999 by Philip Booth. Reprinted by permission of Viking Penguin, a division of Penguin Group (USA) Inc.

Wesley McNair: "Driving North in Winter," from *Fire* by Wesley McNair. Copyright © 2002 by Wesley McNair. Reprinted by permission of David R. Godine, Publisher, Inc.

Edna St. Vincent Millay: When the Year Grows Old," copyright © 1917, 1945, by Edna St. Vincent Millay. Reprinted by permission of Elizabeth Barnett, Literary Executor and The Millay Society.

May Sarton: "The House in Winter," copyright © 1966 by May Sarton, from *Collected Poems 1930–1993* by May Sarton. Reprinted by permission of W.W. Norton & Company, Inc.

For Kathleen

Contents

Spring

Chicken House

Carolyn Page

We feel the old excitement
as we cipher, sketch and reckon:
board feet, pitch of roof so snow will slide.
We're going to build again.

In the greys and whites of winter,
we study catalogs—dream of glistening
tails and fleshy combs,
the strut of rooster, cackle of hen—
their cluck and hustle,
their fierce preoccupation
with perch and pecking order,
and their perfect ovals
saffron-yolked from ranging.

We fell the cedars, strip
their skins down to the silk,
then notch and plate,
plumb and frame our dream,
as in the longing twilight
our hammers sing the nails home.

Spring Peepers

Robert Siegel

Listen, as the cries of spring peepers
like ghostly minnows
swim this way, now that, through
the naked woods,
moonfish seeking their home.

The moon's pale laquearia
flashes upon the water,
the peeping is more insistent,
a whistling tide.
The deep croak of the elders underpins it—

the lime green, the light brown,
the dark green bull with his red earrings
hidden in the murk.
This amphibious symphony
shakes the roots of trees and the nervous buds,

lifts them toward the hologram of stars.
Shrill notes rinse the hollow rocks,
cleanse the hidden waters
running where streams
suck them to the deep ocean.

The frog hibernates in the heart,
come spring, awakens,
leaps and leaps,
sending his laser cries into the blood.
We sleep with short galvanic twitches,

dream of falling,
wake to moonlight burning along the floor,
spilling over the windowsill,
and follow barefoot into the grasses,
our pajama legs soaking up the dew,

down to the edge of the lawn
where the rain makes the ground unsteady,
the thirsty ear drinking in
these arias, duets, choruses,
these nightlong operas, oratorios

of swamp and woods,
these litanies of ascending summer,
from the intimate, singing ventricles of the heart.

Broken Bough

Thomas Carper

The tree will flourish, as the spring intends.
A large limb ice storms broke will not be missed.
After such wrecks of winter, nature mends
The mendable and crosses off her list
What now is just an obstacle in the yard.
So, making space for flourishing grass and flowers,
I cut branches for firewood and discard
The smallest ones as no concern of ours.
Then, after stacking logs where they will dry,
I get a rake to rake the garden clean,
Wondering with a sudden sadness why,
As if not warned about their fate, the green
Buds on forsaken twig-ends still are trying
To come, somehow, to bloom—to keep from dying.

The Saint of Returnables
Elizabeth Tibbetts

Our saint of returnables is back, riding, slow
mile after mile, along the spring roadside,
baskets strapped to his old bike, plastic bags
hung from the handlebars. His gaze averts
to the ditch as he watches for what glitters,
each bottle and can he picks a nickel towards
sustenance. He pedals March through November,
through good and God-awful weather, claiming
what's been tossed out or lost until his bike
is as packed as a mule. When he glances up
we see his face full-on, a face expression
has been erased from, so he looks as though
he has lost his own story somewhere down the road.
But what looks simple could be a twisting path
that would lead to a man's heart. Not the tough
muscle pumping spring air to his thighs, but
that imagined space of the soul, where he stores
everything, and watches, and waits for what's
to come. Yet we're already done, having driven fast
past him—past wood frogs' muttering talk

and blackbirds' red-winged flashes in alders,
past swatches of witch grass and day lilies, leaves
so fierce they push up green inches every day.

Civilities
Philip Booth

Kids in the city, where
there are only dogs, all
the time yelling it.
The same as country kids
yell, trying to be
tough; or women, proving
they have the same right
as men. Rich men pretending
they farm. None of them
within range of my grandmother,
whose proud Victorian bowels
never grumbled, who knew
right words, and which
to use when.
                    When Mr. Bowden
brought to her garden
cartloads of spring dressing,
it was presented, and
billed, as such. In her
presence, horse manure
was not a phrase he'd think

to use. Not that he didn't,
being from up in The County,
know deer droppings from
moosescat, or bearscat
from fox-sign.
                    Fifty years gone,
this tilt backyard is still weighed
by their presence: Mr. Bowden
and Mrs. Hooke, bald pate
and ample bosom, their joined
civilities out inspecting
the edged border of her
perennial garden—the same
garden I'm just about to
turn over for turnips, beets,
and squash, being myself,
in the quick of spring,
already up to my boottops
in the back of the pickup,
forking out to my wife
lovely dark clods of cowdung.

Summer

Fishing

Martin Steingesser

> *"Sometimes words come hard—they resist me*
> *till I pluck them from deep water like hooked fish…"*
> —Lu Ji (261-303)

        You have to be willing
to wait days and days with nothing
biting.
      Wait

while the far leaves, the sky change
blues and greens, and birdcalls,
wind, river become the sound of thinking.
This line you cast
        reaches into different music.

A murmur flutters over the water—
        be more still . . .

Sometimes a moment happens
                        when what moves
doesn't, when the trees and grasses
along the riverbank seem to hold their breath,
and it is the stones that breathe . . .

                        The fish you want
is rising in another world.

The Dragonfly
Louise Bogan

You are made of almost nothing
But of enough
To be great eyes
And diaphanous double vans;
To be ceaseless movement,
Unending hunger
Grappling love.

Link between water and air,
Earth repels you.
Light touches you only to shift into iridescence
Upon your body and wings.

Twice-born, predator,
You split into the heat.
Swift beyond calculation or capture
You dart into the shadow
Which consumes you.

You rocket into the day.
But at last, when the wind flattens the grasses,
For you, the design and purpose stop.

And you fall
With the other husks of summer.

Young Pine

Carl Little

The white pine that happened to grow
needles-to-clapboard at the back of the shed
looks as if it is hiding

from the cops or a gang
or is simply playing hide-and-seek,
a nine-year-old girl, say,

with gentle boughs
hugging the corner of the outbuilding,
trembling in a breeze, hoping

no one notices her until
she can reach a size where the house owner
won't consider her

spindly enough to be cut down.
Lithe, small, hidden,
the young pine is beautiful.

Someone should embrace her
as she grows toward the roofline,
save her from the saw.

Sometimes
Kate Barnes

at night, as I drive up
the dark field-track,
I see,
suddenly,
something so
small in the headlights, so
distant, a delicate, gray
shape that bounds off
toward the drop of the gully;
                and then
there's another . . . and another . . . and
then it's the three does pausing
to look back as they reach
the stone wall,
          and it's
myself caught in the flash
of their eyes, the course
of six gentle, luminous, green
planets under the wide field
of summer stars.

Whale at Twilight

Elizabeth Coatsworth

The sea is enormous, but calm with evening and sunset,
rearranging its islands for the night, changing
                                    its ocean blues,
smoothing itself against the reefs, without playfulness,
                                    without thought.
No stars are out, only sea birds flying to distant reefs.
No vessels intrude, no lobstermen haul their pots,
only somewhere out toward the horizon a thin column
                                    of water appears
and disappears again, and then rises once more,
tranquil as a fountain in a garden where no wind blows.

Fall

September Staying

Patricia Ranzoni

The air is made of missing:
spaces where you were, sounds
lacking yours. A robin basks
on the arbor appreciating as much
as I, and whole bubbles of butterflies
bounce in the garden quiet but for
crickets nearby, crows far off,
leaves high up. Certain flies buzz
somewhere. The spider still weaves
in the hops vine but hummingbirds
have gone, like summerfolk, like you,
to other worlds leaving hardy ones
to season ourselves in stillness again
to find our own peace. Our own place.

Fog Moves In

Gary Lawless

fog moves in behind the island.
seasons, changing.
everything comes and goes.
near dusk, the horses walk to the gate.
I want to sit in the yellow
light of the kitchen,
leaves falling, wind and
fog.

Vespers
Theodore Enslin

That time in the early evening,
a cold sunset gone—
colder than I remember
a year ago
       at apparently
the same time—
the time when cars
go by, one after another.
Purposeful, not speeding,
just to get home.
My neighbors are tired
And hungry.
       For what
do they hunger?
beyond a break in the day,
in from the cold?
       A warm dinner.
What more do they want?

Where do they turn?
Words fail.
They cannot tell me.
If they could
I would not hear them
going past
                down
this ordinarily quiet road.

The House on the Hill

E. A. Robinson

They are all gone away,
    The House is shut and still,
There is nothing more to say.

Through broken walls and gray
    The winds blow bleak and shrill:
They are all gone away.

Nor is there one to-day
    To speak them good or ill:
There is nothing more to say.

Why is it then we stray
    Around the sunken sill?
They are all gone away,

And our poor fancy-play
    For them is wasted skill:
There is nothing more to say.

There is ruin and decay
    In the House on the Hill:
They are all gone away,
There is nothing more to say.

When the Year Grows Old

Edna S. Vincent Millay

I cannot but remember
　　When the year grows old—
October—November—
　　How she disliked the cold!

She used to watch the swallows
　　Go down across the sky,
And turn from the window
　　With a little sharp sigh.

And often when the brown leaves
　　Were brittle on the ground,
And the wind in the chimney
　　Made a melancholy sound,

She had a look about her
　　That I wish I could forget—
The look of a scared thing
　　Sitting in a net!

Oh, beautiful at nightfall
    The soft spitting snow!
And beautiful the bare boughs
    Rubbing to and fro!

But the roaring of the fire,
    And the warmth of fur,
And the boiling of the kettle
    Were beautiful to her!

I cannot but remember
    When the year grows old—
October—November—
    How she disliked the cold!

Winter

Snow-Flakes

Henry Wadsworth Longfellow

Out of the bosom of the Air,
    Out of the cloud-folds of her garments shaken,
Over the woodlands brown and bare,
    Over the harvest-fields forsaken,
        Silent, and soft, and slow
        Descends the snow.

Even as our cloudy fancies take
    Suddenly shape in some divine expression,
Even as the troubled heart doth make
    In the white countenance confession,
        The troubled sky reveals
        The grief it feels.

This is the poem of the air,
    Slowly in silent syllables recorded;
This is the secret of despair,
    Long in its cloudy bosom hoarded,
        Now whispered and revealed
        To wood and field.

The House in Winter

May Sarton

The house in winter creaks like a ship.
Snow-locked to the sills and harbored snug
In soft white meadows, it is not asleep.
When icicles pend on the low roof's lip,
The shifting weight of a slow-motion tug
May slide off sometimes in a crashing slip.
At zero I have heard a nail pop out
From clapboard like a pistol shot.

All day this ship is sailing out on light:
At dawn we wake to rose and amber meadows,
At noon plunge on across the waves of white,
And, later, when the world becomes too bright,
Tack in among the lengthening blue shadows
To anchor in black-silver pools of night.
Although we do not really come and go,
It feels a long way up and down from zero.

At night I am aware of life aboard.
The scampering presences are often kind,

Leaving under a cushion a seed-hoard,
But I can never open any cupboard
Without a question: what shall I find?
A hard nut in my boot? An apple cored?
The house around me has become an ark
As we go creaking on from dark to dark.

There is a wilder solitude in winter
When every sense is pricked alive and keen
For what may pop or tumble down or splinter.
The light itself, as active as a painter,
Swashes bright flowing banners down
The flat white walls. I stand here like a hunter
On the *qui vive*, although all appears quite calm,
And feel the silence gather like a storm.

Starting the Subaru at Five Below

Stuart Kestenbaum

After 6 Maine winters and 100,000 miles,
when I take it to be inspected

I search for gas stations where they
just say beep the horn and don't ask me to

put in on the lift, exposing its soft
rusted underbelly. Inside is the record

of commuting: apple cores, a bag from
McDonald's, crushed Dunkin' Donuts cups,

a flashlight that doesn't work and one
that does, gas receipts blurred beyond

recognition. Finger tips numb, nose
hair frozen, I pump the accelerator

and turn the key. The battery cranks,
the engine gives 2 or 3 low groans and

starts. My God it starts. And unlike
my family in the house, the job I'm

headed towards, the poems in my briefcase,
the dreams I had last night, there is

no question about what makes sense.
White exhaust billowing from the tail pipe,

heater blowing, this car is going to
move me, it's going to take me places.

Kitchen

Kristin Linquist

There is the ritual of icing the sugar cookies,
the sacrament of eating them:
sheep, reindeer, turkey, tree, little man.
There is the prayer of the old pressed tin ceiling,
litany of the clock with its waxing moon face,
blessing of the cast-iron potbelly stove
fragrant with coffee and rising bread.
The hymn of certain knowledge.
The psalm of bringing it back.

Driving North in Winter

Wesley McNair

All the way to Mercer these
rooms left out
in the dark—

lamplight and two chairs
the old couple sit
reading in,

a table where a family
comes together
for dinner—

the rest of the houses, one
with the night. How
blessed they are,

the man hanging his ordinary
coat in the small world
of a kitchen,

the woman turning to her cupboard,
both of them held
from the cold

and the vastness by nothing
but trusting
inattention

and one beam of light,
like us passing by
in the darkness,

you napping, me wide awake
and grateful for this
moment

we've also been given, apart
in our way of being
together, living

in the light.